The Motivated Leader

How to bring back motivation for Early Years Leaders

Sarah Putland

The Motivated Leader

How to bring back motivation for Early Years Leaders

By Sarah Putland

Introduction

My name is Sarah and in my spare time, I am a lover of being organised, having things aesthetically pleasing, spending time in nature, walking my dogs, and enjoying the changing of the seasons and rhythms of the year.

I have worked in early years for around 17 years, originally a qualified teacher in an infants school and a special needs school, then moving on to purchasing my own day nursery in 2005.

Recently I have seen how so many nursery managers and EYFS leaders have become deflated, with a loss of motivation and love for their job. The past few years especially have been so tough for us in early years; having to deal with a pandemic, changes to the EYFS, increasing costs, and to top it all off, a recruitment crisis within the sector. Our days now, are more about 'survival' rather than about why we took the job in the first place. I have written this book as I

Introduction

want to find a way to support leaders and managers in the early years to get their motivation back and reignite their passion to make each day worthwhile. I want to share my experience and help you to create a calmer, more productive approach to your job role. Finding time to fit everything in, that you need to do in a day, and to look after yourself too. You may be new to the job role, or maybe an existing leader or manager, that needs some support to get their love back for early years. Whatever your situation is, I am hoping that this book will help you.

When you train to complete your level 3 qualification, you learn how to work with the children in your settings, how to observe and plan for children. You then work your way up in your career path. Once you get to a room leader role, you start to be responsible for a staff team, something that was not covered in your level 3 qualification. Then once you hit manager level, there is not an instruction booklet, to guide you through all the new responsibilities that you now have. Having to deal with administrative tasks, budgets, staff supervisions and professional development, dealing with complaints and being in charge of all the policies and procedures- the list is endless and all these things are new to you. As an EYFS lead in a school, you would have trained to support the children with their learning, but not how to deal with situations in a leadership role and how to support your staff team. Unless you do training in leadership and management, you might not know 'where to start,'

Introduction

or the best way to tackle things, your current knowledge may only be what you have observed others do. I am hoping this book will help you. This book will take you on a journey by looking at the different skills that leaders need as well as looking at your own well-being, where your passions lie, and how to support and inspire your staff teams.

My nursery is a very large nursery and can take 115 children at one time. We take children from babies until they start school. Within this book I will share with you, how my own setting was a loud and busy place to work and how it became calmer and happier. Day to day life is still busy and some days are a lot harder than others, but it's about having those strategies and good teamwork around you, that will help you get through those days.

Before I began this journey my days were busy- everything was at a fast pace. Room leaders needed to have a few hours a week to plan, this time then needed to be 'covered' in the rooms and by the time they had finished their planning, it was time for them to start all over again! So many jobs needed to be done within a day. It felt like we never had the time to actually be with the children.

Being a hands-on owner, I was always working. Even when I was not at the nursery, I would spend time in the evenings completing paperwork and then in the nursery at weekends, tidying up the rooms, and moving them about to look nicer. I was missing out

Introduction

on special time with my family and work/ life balance was non-existent.

My to do list was ever increasing.

One day I realised that I wanted more for my setting, for my staff team, for the children and families that attended the nursery. I was lucky enough to have a great management team, who were also feeling the same as me. I started researching different learning approaches and different ways of leading practise in education. There had to be something that was more child centred and that allowed the practitioners to be with the children more. I then came across 'The Curiosity Approach.'

'The Curiosity Approach is a modern day approach to Early Childhood. It was founded by Stephanie Bennett and Lyndsey Hellyn. They wanted their approach to motivate educators to be passionate and curious professionals, who in turn provide wonderous opportunities for children.'

www.thecuriosityapproach.com

This approach takes elements from other educational approaches such as Montessori (learning life skills and independence), Reggio Emilia (having the child at the centre of everything we do, listening to 100 languages of children), Te Whāriki (having a sense of belonging), Steiner (Changing of the seasons, bringing nature into play and the routines and rhythms of the day), and Emmi Pikler (the natural

Introduction

unfolding child). It also included elements of Hyyge and Zen.

As a setting we then embarked on our journey to complete our accreditation. The journey made a huge impact on our setting, and we quickly began to see the atmosphere calming down, the practitioners having the time to interact with the children more and the children becoming so much more engaged.

While on this journey, I started to do my own research on leadership and management skills and different methods. There are many different learning approaches out there for you to follow if you wish to, but there isn't a specific leadership and management approach for our sector. I wanted to take elements of different leadership approaches and create one that would work for us, alongside the Curiosity Approach.

The last few years especially have been tough on education. Working through a pandemic has had such an impact on everybody and we have all had to work even harder than normal. We have all felt the strain and stress of this and as leaders and managers we have not only had to look after ourselves but keep the well-being of our staff teams and families in our constant thoughts. We were not given any extra praise or recognition by the outside world, for carrying on and trying to bring some normality to our families and children that we work with daily. We were all feeling de-motivated.

Introduction

By putting new leadership strategies in place, we began to see a difference. The nursery felt calm, and there was a good sense of team work.

Creating change is always hard and is always met with difficulties. But it can work and have a huge positive impact on your day to day lives.

If these situations sound familiar to you, then I am hoping that this book can help you.

Whether you are an existing manager or an EYFS lead, and the last few years have left you feeling exhausted and deflated, or whether you are new to the role and would like some tips and support on how to lead your team, then I am hoping this book can help you.

Within this book I will talk you through the different stages in order to become an 'ultimate leader' within the early years. Each chapter will discuss a different area from what I think is the perfect leadership and management approach. Following this approach will give you motivation, and to be able to motivate and inspire your staff team. It will enable you to look after your own well-being as well as that of your staff team, and will also include a day to day organisation system that you can follow in order to give you more time to carry out the aspects of the job that you love.

If you follow the strategies and ideas that I have set out in this book, then I am hoping that you will find your passion again. Not only that, but your staff team

Introduction

will also have the opportunity to be motivated again too. Some of the suggestions in this book may come across as unnecessary but combining everything together should have impact on your setting or school and most importantly, on you too.

Chapter 1
Starting with yourself

"One of the most important actions/ things a leader can do, is to lead by example. If you want everyone else to be passionate, committed, dedicated, and motivated, you go first!"

Marshall Goldsmith

For many years I worked on average, 60 hours per week. I was in my setting most of everyday and then would continue paperwork at home, in the evenings and at weekends. I would also make time to go into the nursery at weekends too. A long bank holiday for me was exciting because I could get lots of physical things done at nursery while it was empty! It wasn't seen, back then, as a time to spend with family. I'm sure this sounds familiar to a lot of you. Then a few years ago, a few stressful events happened all at the same time and my body gave up and crashed. I was then diagnosed with Myalgic Encephalomyelitis (M.E / Chronic fatigue syndrome) and Fibromyalgia. I had pushed my body too far for many years and this was the result of not looking after myself. I then found myself in a position where I had to make life changes, otherwise my body just simply wouldn't work. I knew my mind had lots to give, but I was at the point of exhaustion and didn't know how I was going to get back into a positive mindset. I had my dreams that I wanted to fulfil but I had to change my mindset and way of life in order to be able to carry on doing a job that I had loved and wanted to love again.

In this chapter, we are starting with you. It is so important that you look after yourself first before you can even begin to think of leading others. Don't do what I did- you need to change your mindset now before it's too late.

Understanding, that if I wanted to continue doing the leadership role that I loved, I came across the book 'Rhythm of Life' by Matthew Kelly.

Matthew Kelly talks about the different needs that people have and how you must live each day in order to be 'the best version of yourself.'

You need to look at your legitimate needs as physical, emotional, intellectual, and spiritual. Take a minute to think about these 4 areas in your current life – which ones are you thriving in now and which ones are you neglecting, as you do not see them as urgent?

In order to have the strength to lead and motivate your staff team, you need to concentrate on yourself. You need to make sure you are looking after your own health and mind as a priority. As the Curiosity Approach gets us to think about the routines and rhythm of the day with our children. I want you to start to think about your own rhythm and routines as a leader.

Go through each section below and make a note of what you currently do under each heading and set yourselves some goals for what you need to do.

If you would like to use the format that I have created, then please email me sarah@sarahputlandearlyyearsconsultancy.co.uk and put 'Book Downloads' as the subject.

Physical needs

We all know that we have primary needs to live. We need to breath, eat and drink to survive. We also have secondary needs that are not critical to our survival but essential if we want to succeed and do well. These needs are things such as physical exercise and a healthy diet. These are the things that we can neglect if we are living a busy and stressful life, where we do not make the time. On a busy day, you may not take a break, you might not have time to eat your lunch, or probably be so tired when you get home, that you go for the quick option of processed food or take away. Being healthy is not always our first priority.

Think of ways that you can maintain your physical needs. How do you spend your days off? Do you continue to do work at home or have your emails on your phone so can keep checking them. Or do you allow your mind to break free of work. I have now trained myself to use the 'out of office' notification on emails. We all need that time to be free from the thinking of work. Do you use your 'out of office' as part of your weekly routine? We live in a society where everything is instant. A parent emailing you or another professional, may give you the pressure to respond instantly, but if they receive your 'out of office' or perhaps a different response such as 'I will endeavour to respond to your email within 1-2 working days', this takes the pressure off you to do things instantaneously.

Walking in nature is a great way to relieve any stress that you have or to clear your mind. I love walking my dogs and although my energy levels and activity time is limited each day, I make this a priority for my own mental health. Steiner talks about the importance of children being out in nature and experiencing the changes in the seasons. This can also be good for us, as adults too. No matter what the weather, I take a walk in nature each day. Sometimes it is for only a short length of time, but it is important no matter the length of time. How far away do you live from your work? Can you walk to work instead of driving? My staff team set up a walking group between them and meet outside of work to go for different walks together, encouraging each other. I think this is a fantastic idea and love seeing the photos of where they have been.

When you are at work, do you take breaks from your desk? Do you find yourself eating your lunch and working? Instead leave the building and get some fresh air, take a walk around the block. At the moment you might not even take a break. You need to prioritise yourself.

In our setting we changed the way we did our staff breaks. Our staff all eat their lunch with the children, making this a special time within the setting. Staff then have their breaks later in the afternoon so that time is theirs to spend how they want, and they don't have the pressure of rushing their food. Even if they choose to have a 20-minute break, some sit in peace with a hot drink for that time, some read, some sit outside, or some go for a walk…. It gives them the chance to unwind in their own way. In early years our days are long, and breaks are short, so you need to make sure you use the time well. Make it a priority to look at how you take your break and what you do in this time for your own self-care. Look at how you maintain your physical health and your diet.

Give yourself a goal of something you want to try over the next month. Write it down!

Emotional needs

If we neglect our emotional needs, it is not life threatening, but can lead to unhappiness, depression, mood swings and general lethargy. This prevents us from being 'the best version of ourselves.' Spending time with different people; with your family, your friends, your partner, helps you to fulfil your emotional needs. This is the one area that I realised I was neglecting for all those years. It is so important to get a work / life balance. If you are finding yourself, on your day off, feeling like you can't be bothered to do anything else apart from watch a boxset on Netflix, then you need to address your emotional needs. Give yourself a goal to meet up with different friends or take time out to do something fun with your family or take up a hobby. Netflix can then be your reward!

As part of ensuring we meet our emotional needs, we need to also feel like we have a sense of belonging. This could be being part of a friendship group or being part of your family unit. We also need to have a sense of belonging within our workplace. (We will look more into being part of a team in chapter 5).

Set yourself a goal of something that you want to do over the next month, that will support your emotional needs. Write it down!

Intellectual needs.

We need ideas that inspire us, challenge us, stretch our minds, show us what is possible and encourage us to want to do better.

The thought of professional development can excite some people, but for others that are feeling exhausted and feel like they have no time, professional development is pushed aside. It is so important to find a way that professional development can excite you. It can help you on your journey of where you want to go. Just the fact that you are reading this book is an excellent starting point- you want to motivate yourself and be the 'best version of you.' You want help in how to achieve your goals.

Just like our bodies need regular exercise to keep healthy, so do our minds. This is the area that I can support you with further. Later, in this chapter, I will help you to set yourselves some goals for your professional development. Professional development can give us the motivation that we need, to reignite our passion and love for our jobs.

Spiritual needs

Each of us have a different spiritual journey and have different needs. According to Matthew Kelly we all have 3 things that we need in our spiritual lives: silence, solitude and simplicity. The way we seek these are all different.

When working through our accreditation with the Curiosity Approach, I discovered how to incorporate Zen and Hygge into our settings each day. Researching more into these, made me look at my own personal life and how I could include these for myself, at home and at work. I created a special place in my house (just a corner in one room) that is my 'go to place.' When I am feeling exhausted or stressed, I go to this space to have some silence and alone time (although I tend to always have a dog or 3 with me!) I have placed certain things in this space such as a nice cushion, a blanket, place for my mug of tea (or wine glass!) etc. Have you got a special place that you can retreat to away from the hustle and bustle of daily life? If you have small children, it might be a place you go to for a little while when they are in bed. Try thinking of a space that you could develop.

I wake up each morning half an hour before I need to so that I have some peaceful time with a cup of tea before the madness in our house starts. I love to read and so this is my time of day to do just that. I always start the day reading an inspiring book, with a pot of tea. This has made a big impact on my daily routine as there is no longer that mad rush. With my energy levels being limited each day, this has been an important part in my daily routine. I wrote most of this book during this time of day. It is a good time of day for me for reflection. When is your best time of day?

Having time in silence and solitude gives you time to reflect. You may find this easier to do at the end of the day. Clearing your mind at the end of the day is so important to be able to sleep better and to not keep thinking of work. (We talk more about how to carry out a 'mind sweep' later in the book)

What goal can you set yourself over the month, to help with your spiritual needs?

Now that you have read about these four areas, you should have set yourself some goals for your personal development. You now have a starting point. You should have some actions under three of the above headings that you need to make time to achieve.

I suggested to set yourself monthly goals, but you can change the time frame to meet your own needs. At the end of each month reflect on how this has gone and set new goals.

Now we can look further into your intellectual needs for you to set yourself some goals in this area.

What does it take to succeed?

Maybe you are new to a manager's or leader position and want some support, or you have been a manager / year group leader for a while and need some inspiration. Have you found yourself getting excited about an idea but then things pop up in your way and you then feel that you do not have the time or energy to follow it through?

I know what it is like when you are on a role with a development, then something happens such as a complaint from a parent. This has such an impact on everybody and especially the manager/ leader. It is so hard to pick up the energy levels that you had on something beforehand.

Do you find that you are constantly telling yourself that you cannot achieve something? "I don't have time to do that?" "The budget won't allow for that to happen?" "My team will not agree with my ideas?"

There are ways around all these problems, but you need to have the positive mindset. Try changing the wording in your thought process. Change your 'don'ts' to 'dos' and your 'cant's' to 'I cans.'

There are two types of stress. One is due to a change happening that makes it harder for you to get something done, a disruption in routine or circumstance. For example, a staff member calling in sick, so you now need to spend some of the day in a room. This means that you now won't have time to get a report done or reply to an email. This can cause you stress short term. If this continues to happen, then this short-term stress can start to become long term stress. It comes about from not having job fulfilment. You are stuck in a role that limits your creativity and it doesn't satisfy you anymore. This is known as chronic stress. If you have this, then the short-term stress situations start to become overwhelming. You may be thinking that this is how you are currently feeling in your role, and you do not know what to do in order to get out of it. You may even be thinking that this job is no longer for you as you cannot see how it will improve. There is hope, don't worry.

Just like we learn that all our children are unique, we as adults, are too. We all have different talents, strengths, and skills that we can bring to our role. But what is our purpose? When we are feeling tired and overwhelmed, our inner critic voice can be heard. This voice can be:

- Critical and harsh to us
- Gives us lots of reasons why we can't be successful or do well
- It listens to the negativity in our lives
- It only focus' on problems and not solutions

However, we also have an inner mentor voice inside of us, that can be a lot quieter for us to hear. This voice can:

- Give us support and encouragement
- Can be forward moving
- Can think of possibilities and potential

We need to find a way to get our inner mentor voice to be louder in our heads. So, what is your speciality? What are your skills and talents? Let's find out……

The first place to start is to figure out where your passion lies? What inspires you? What motivates you? You need to figure out what your heart screams out for you to do. Then work out how this can be incorporated into your leader role.

To do this, you need to work through the following questions:

(Grab a hot drink, find a quiet space, get comfy and work through these questions)

1. Think about times in your life that were your happiest moments? Why? Think about what made you feel this way and how you could feel that way again. Some of my happiest times (accept my wedding day and my children being born of course!) have been when I have worked hard and achieved something such as my degree and my master's degree. That sense of achievement makes it worthwhile and that is what inspires me.
2. Write a list of adjectives that you would like people to use when describing you. This will give you a sense of what type of leader you would want to be.
3. What would you like to be remembered for? What impact would you like to have on your current nursery or school? What would you like people to say about you?
4. Ask your friends or staff team to tell you one thing that you are absolutely the best at.

5. If you had to be interviewed to talk about something that you are interested in for a certain length of time, what would you talk about and why? What would you be able to talk about, from the heart?
6. Who are the ten people you admire most and why? These could be celebrities, colleagues, friends etc.
7. What upsets you the most in the world? Do you have any ideas on how to make it better? For example, I get upset with our school system and how we should be planning a more child centred approach. When I start talking about this, I feel my passion coming through!
8. What makes you stand out from other people? Why are you a good manager / leader compared to others. What specific skills have you got that you can offer?
9. What specific skills have you developed that make you successful at what you do? Think about any professional development that you may have completed recently. Have you got any specific skills that support you in your role?
10. What makes you happy when you are at work? Think about the aspects of your job role and which parts you enjoy more than others.
11. What activities make you lose all sense of time? Which aspects of your job role do you enjoy the most?

From these questions, look through your answers and work out what inspires you and gets you motivated. This is where we need to begin. Can any of this be brought into your job role? For example, you might realise that setting up the learning environment is something that makes you lose all sense of time, but it is something that you do not have time to do now. How can you bring this into your job role as a leader? Can you support your team to do this? Can you lead training on it? Try and think of a way to bring the things that motivate you, into your job role.

I bet for many of you, your average week does not include any of the things that you enjoy doing. Other jobs are always seen as more important and so your strengths are not being used how they should be.

Now make a list of the different types of jobs that you carry out in a normal average week. Once you have done this, add any jobs that you need to carry out each month in addition to your weekly tasks.

For example, you may have the following tasks:

- Answering emails to parents / professionals / colleagues
- Showing prospective parents around
- Answering staff questions
- Answering the phone
- Filing paperwork

- Working out staffing levels / cover for sickness
- Supervisions
- Preparing for staff meeting
- Covering breaks

Now next to each job, put how many hours per week, on average you spend on this type of job.

I bet that being on your computer (Jobs such as answering emails, typing up paperwork or reports, working out staffing etc) was quite high on the amount of time you spend each week. According to Richard Nelson Bolles (2012) a study that was carried out in the same year found that the average person spent around 30% of their working week just on reading and answering emails. This was 10 years ago, so I am imagining it to be a lot higher now.

If this type of job is a high percentage of your working week, think about the following:

- Is it necessary to answer emails straight away (use your out of office)
- Can you share access to your emails so that it is not always down to you to respond? For example, do you have a deputy that can take over for a day to release you to do something else? Can your emails be forwarded to other colleagues to answer?
- If you are finding that you are the only one available to answer the emails that come

through, then we talk later in the book, about selecting certain times that you only check and answer emails.
- Think about having a technology free day. Let everyone know, for example, on a Friday I will not be based in my office and not answering any emails. Instead use the day to spend on the part of your job that you enjoy and love. This might be spending time in a room and observing or carrying out a project that you have been wanting to complete for a long time. The team around you and parents will soon get used to your new routine. Try it!

From the list that you created above, highlight the things that you really enjoy doing (let's hope that there is some!) What is it about these jobs? For example, you might be someone that likes to lead staff in a new development, or you may prefer the problem-solving aspect of your job. Everyone is different but it's important for you to spend time doing what you enjoy to love your job and have the motivation each day.

The purpose of these exercises was to make you think of the things in your job role that you really enjoy. You may also have other skills that you want to develop further but you have not been able to bring into your job role yet as you have never found the time. Now is your chance. Think about whether you need to spend the amount of time you do each week on certain jobs. Are these always relevant or a priority to complete? Can they be delegated to other people in your team? The idea is to re-adjust your role so that you spend time doing the things you enjoy more and this in turn will make the other jobs more bearable.

If you would like to look further into this, then we look at this in more detail within module one of 'The Ultimate Early Years Leader' programme. This course and other support materials can be found on my website:

www.sarahputlandearlyyearsconsultancy.co.uk

In order to develop your intellectual needs, you need to set yourself some professional development goals. Think about where you are currently. Why are you in this role? You may have chosen to become a manager or a leader, or you may have been put in this position and not sure where to begin. You might be frustrated or deflated at the moment. Be honest with yourself and write it down.

The next thing you need to do is give yourself a one year goal. This goal is for you professionally (we are not looking at the setting yet). What do you really want to achieve? It might be to lead an outstanding setting. It might be to achieve a qualification in a certain area.

Think about why this is important to you to achieve? It could be to improve your 'work / life' balance, or to feel happier in your job. Whatever it is- why is it important? Break your yearly goal down into smaller monthly goals. What do you need to achieve these goals? Some training in a certain area might be needed. Or you may need to rethink your daily / weekly routine in order to change your work / life balance. It might be having the time. Whatever your goal is, there may be something you need to do to achieve it. It is so important to make this part of your daily/ weekly actions so that it **can** be achieved. We talk about this in more detail in chapter 7.

It can be achieved! You need to give yourself a positive mindset that this goal will be achieved, by you, in a year's time. You just need to work out the plan to achieve it.

As human beings we all need to look after ourselves in the four areas: physical, emotional, intellectual, and spiritual. Always remember that you are not as strong as you think – I learnt this the hard way.

Your life needs to be filled with happiness, success, and inspiration. It should be lived passionately. You need to know your needs.

By the time you have worked through this chapter, I am hoping that you now have a plan of action in place for you to move forward. Well done on completing the first stage.

Chapter Summary:

- To look at where you are currently at under the four areas: physical, emotional, intellectual, and spiritual. Which area do you need to work on? Set yourself some actions
- What is your passion? What gets that 'fire in your belly?'
- Where are you currently at? What is stopping you now
- Set yourself a one-year goal? Think about why this is important to you.
- How will you achieve this goal? Come up with an action plan so that you know what you need to do to achieve this.

Chapter 2
What type of leader are you?

"A boss has the title, A leader has the people"

Simon Sinek

Our job can cause our anxiety levels and stress levels to rise - why do we feel like this? The answer simply is because we care. We care about the setting or school that we work in. So, when things are not going according to plan, or you do not get the time to get things done- you worry, and this then causes you anxiety and stress. We all go into work with an idea in our head of how we want the day to go, however, a typical day for us could be:

- 7:30am Come into work
- 7:40am Get a phone call from a member of staff who is unwell

(This then causes you to have to think on the spot about how to maintain ratios and how you are going to cover this)

- 8-9am Meet and greet children and parents with a smile on your face (inside you are still trying to solve the last problem)
- 9am Problem solve and sort out staffing in all rooms
- 9:30am Check emails and deal with any emergencies.
- 10am Solve a problem for the cook, a teacher, or fix the photocopier,
- 10:30am Sit at your desk to answer some emails to realise you only have half an hour now before you must go and cover everyone's lunch breaks

(If you are an early year's manager you could be covering lunch breaks from as early as 11 until 2 or maybe later! This is almost one third of your day and working week!)

- 2pm Remember to finally eat!
- 2:30pm Get back in your office to continue checking emails from before
- 3pm There is a problem with tea- so back up to problem solve
- 4pm Back to your office
- 5pm Back out to see the children out with another smile on your face.

- 5:30pm to the kitchen to wash up as your member of staff has had to go home unwell
- 6pm End of your day!

You can see from the above example, how many different hats you must wear over a typical day, how many different things you need to think about and how the time just runs away with you. I may have slightly exaggerated above, but I am sure you can relate to days like this. How are we meant to get things done and develop our staff teams? This ends up with us feeling demotivated and in turn demotivates your team. Over the course of a day, you deal with so many different situations and I bet you have never thought about the different types of leader roles you can be in one day.

We have spent some time looking at your individual needs. Now we will start to look at how you can support and lead your team, creating an inspiring atmosphere which in turn motivates your staff and will then motivate you.

What type of leader are you?

Below I have described some different types of leaders (these are not all the types; I have selected the most common types for our sector):

Authoritarian

This is a leader that likes to take control over everyone and everything. They have overall control on decision making and don't involve any staff members.

Positives

It could produce consistent results.

It reduces the amount of time needed to make a decision. All the pressure is on the leader so the staff team may feel slightly more relaxed.

Negatives

It could kill creativity within a team and any ideas that the staff may have. Your team won't think for themselves and may cause a bit of team rebellion.

It may also lead you to feeling stressed and 'burnt out.' When you have time off, your team will not know what they should be doing if you have never let them take control at some point.

Having a deputy would be difficult for you, as you do not like to delegate and allow someone else to take control.

Transformational

This is a leader that inspires their team with a vision.

Positives

There may be low staff turnover as it establishes strong relationships.

Vision is so important to high moral. The leader gives their team constant feedback and gives them motivation. The team are therefore able to work without your constant help as they have set goals and know what they are wanting to achieve.

Negatives

A team member may disagree with the vision. This can be hard to deal with.

Smaller issues / jobs within the workplace maybe overlooked as you focus on the vision too much.

May put added pressure onto staff members to get things done. As a leader you could easily slip into the habit of being mainly office based as you are only focusing on one thing. You therefore will not be experiencing what is happening in the rooms. It is important to get this balance right so that the team trust you and your vision.

Participative

This is a leader that involves all team members in decision making.

Positives

It makes a strong team, increases motivation and job satisfaction.

Negatives

You need to be aware, however, that some decisions need to be made quickly and so there may not be time to gain everyone's ideas and thoughts. It's getting to know the correct balance. It may also lead to poor decision making based on the experience of your team.

This way of leading is easier when you only have a small team but can be difficult to always do with a large team and if you have part time staff.

Transactional

This type of leader likes to give their team rewards for getting things done.

Positives

They give their team SMART targets.

They have an easy-to-understand system and can create a sense of fairness; if you achieve something you get rewarded. If you don't, you don't. This can be achieved through supervisions, for example.

Negatives

If not done correctly, it may cause a lack of focus on getting to know your individual staff members and building a relationship with them.

Difficult to find rewards that motivate all your staff as they are all individuals. You may not have the time to see all your team at even intervals.

Delegative

This type of leader likes to delegate to their team members.

Positives

Staff creativity is highly valued. Leaders create positive environments.

It prevents burn out as you utilise your team members to the work with you or for you. It may also save you time. Your team feel valued when trust them to do something for you.

Negatives

This type of leadership, if not done correctly may end up with poor leadership in a project. It shifts responsibilities onto some team members that may not have the correct experience. Change may not be taken well as there is not a clear sense of leadership.

From the above each type of leader can 'have its place.' Each one has its positives and negatives. What we want to do is try and take the positive aspects from them all to create the 'Ultimate leader' in you.

So, let's work out what type of leader you think you currently are?

Here is a little quiz. Write down which leader you are for each scenario; a-e (If you are not sure which answer to select, then you can select more than one).

1. You have an area you want to develop within your setting or school, do you:

A - Write an action plan of what **you** need to do

B - Sets goals and share them with the team

C - Hold a staff meeting and ask for everyone's ideas on how to move forwards

D - Tell the staff what they need to do and what they will get from doing it

E - Give the project to the team and tell them to work it out for themselves

2. You notice a member of your staff team is demotivated so you.....

A - Follow them around and closely monitor what they are doing

B - Speak to them to let them know they are letting their team down and they have goals to meet

C - Make an extra effort to ensure that they are involved in team discussions and decisions

D - Speak to the member of staff and remind them about what they could achieve and what reward there will be

E - Back away, as they clearly needing space

3. Some of your team are highly skilled and motivated. Do you.....

A - Continue to lead all projects yourself. Your staff are busy so why add to their workload

B - Set each room, goals that they need to achieve in their own way

C - Suggest each team come to you to discuss ideas and agree them together

D - All rooms have to follow the same process

E - Let each team carry out the project in their own way

4. There are a couple of issues between team members.

A - I sit both members of staff down and discuss the problem

B - I remind all staff that we have a vision and goals to meet

C - Ask their team leader what the problem is and what they would like to do

D - Speak to staff members and explain that they are not meeting their targets

E - Separate them so they don't have to work together.

5. How would you ensure that your staff team are working towards your vision and ethos?

A - Lead from the front

B - Have a big emphasis on goal setting to achieve your vision. Nothing else is as important

C - Ask all staff to participate with their own ideas

D - Put a reward system in place for those who achieve their goals

E - Delegate most of the jobs to others in your team

Add up all your answers.

Mostly a's – you are an authoritarian leader

Mostly b's – you are a transformational leader

Mostly c's – you are a participative leader

Mostly d's – you are a transactional leader

Mostly e's – you are a delegative leader

What type of leader are you currently? You may fall into one category, or you may be even across a few. Think about what type of leader you would prefer to be. You might want to have aspects from each of them. Whatever you decide, think about how you can achieve this when dealing with different situations.

When you go to lead practise next or tackle a certain situation try and make a conscience effort to think about which type of leader would be more effective when dealing with the situation.

Chapter summary:

- There are many different types of leaders, each one has its positives and negatives
- What type of leader are you currently and what would you like to be?
- Think about what type of leader would be best in different situations
- Make yourself aware of how you deal with different situations and think beforehand what type of leader you want to be when dealing with it.

Chapter 3
Your Vision as a setting

"Leaders don't force people to follow. They invite them on a journey."

Www.yourpositiveoasis.com

Now that you have more of an understanding where you are going as an individual and what type of leader you would like to be, the next thing to do is to create an atmosphere of 'teamwork.' Setting team goals, together, can help build this. These goals will show you all where you are going as a manager of a setting or a leader of a department.

I believe that one of the most important aspects of being a leader is to set a vision with your team.

What is your vision and what is your why in your setting or school?

When I realised, I had to change my mindset, I knew I had to be really clear about where I wanted to go for my own professional development and why, and also where I wanted my setting to go- what our vision was. This meant I knew what I had to focus on each day, with my limited energy levels.

Giving your setting a clear vision to work towards, guides people's priorities and supports you all in your day-to-day routines.

In Simon Sinek's book, 'Start with Why,' he talks about the golden circle.

Simon Sinek 'The Golden Circle.'

We all know in our settings **what** we are meant to be doing. But let's start with the centre; the '**why**.'

What is your purpose, your reasons, your beliefs, as a setting or a school? Inspired leaders always act from the inside out. They start with the 'why,' then move to the 'how' and then the 'what.' What is your vision as a setting or school, what is your purpose? How will you get there and what do you need to do? You may already have a vision in place, but nobody refers to it or maybe not all staff know what it is. You may have had the same vision for a long time, but times have now changed, and you may feel it is time for a new start. It might be better to start again and this time, involve all your team. This will be when you need to use your 'participative' leader role.

Sinek describes this exercise as a tree. Its roots and trunk represent the foundation of your setting / school. In that tree are branches- those branches are the separate departments within. For example, in a nursery setting the different branches would represent the different age groups. In a school the different branches would represent the different departments such as foundation stage, key stage one etc. On these branches, sit nests. The nests are the different teams or staff members that you have. All of you are working towards keeping the foundations of your tree alive. Your organisations vision. How will you be looking at this, within your role? Will you be developing the roots, the branches, or a nest?

Your first step is to work together to find your 'why.' This is more likely to be done within a staff meeting for your team. Simon Sinek refers to it as 'the tribe approach.' If you are a manager of a setting, this will be your full staff team (setting the foundations of your tree) If you are a leader of a department, or smaller group, this will be for the staff within your department (creating those branches and nests that support the foundation).

Before the meeting ask your staff to think about how they see their vision to be, for your nursery or school? What is their ideal setting? What does it look like, feel like to work there? Ask them to bring along quotes, pictures or just be willing to describe their thoughts verbally.

Plan your staff meeting so you all have the appropriate time to discuss this together. If you are doing this as a full school or setting, then break the teams down into 'departments.' Provide large sheets of paper and pens so that each group can have their own.

Once you have explained what needs to be done, the staff can break up into groups and discuss their views and share any pictures that they may have brought along. When we did this at our setting, we had more visual learners within our team, so I asked everyone to bring along pictures and/or quotes. I wanted our nursery's vision to be visual and displayed around the nursery.

Let the teams have a discussion together. When ready, bring your team back together, take the themes that have emerged from their discussions, discuss together as a whole group, until you have a set of themes that you have all agreed on.

When I did this in my setting, we came up with four themes and placed pictures and quotes under each theme- bringing our 'why' alive for everyone to see.

From this exercise we knew, as a setting, where we were going and what we were working towards.

We came up with the following:

> *'We believe that every child is an individual and through listening to the child's voice, we aim to create curious thinkers through our homely, natural & engaging learning environments.'*

Alongside our mission statement, we have a vision board which is displayed, so that everyone could see what our vision was. Be proud of your vision and display it so that visitors, and parents can see and as a reminder to your team each day.

Once you know your why, you then can start to look at your 'how.' How are you going to achieve this? What things do you need to put in place to achieve your why. For us, it was completing our Curiosity Approach accreditation as we knew this approach was the best learning approach to do this. It maybe that you need to look at an alternative pedagogy or to create your own curriculum. You may realise that your team need some further professional development in order to achieve your vision. Everyone's visions will be different.

If you would like further support, then I offer lots of different bespoke support packages for your nursery or school.

You are now ready to set goals together. What do you want to achieve over the next year? Create a team action plan of how you will achieve this. When doing this remember your different leader roles. Which type will you be when working through the action plans with your team.

Chapter Summary:

- arrange a team meeting and ask your staff to bring pictures, quotes, and ideas as to what their vision is for the setting

- lead a staff meeting to bring all the Ideas together under different themes.

- together write your vision

- put a plan of action in place as to how you will achieve this and what you want to achieve over the next year.

Chapter 4
Managing Change

"Leaders don't force people to follow. They invite them on a journey."

Managing change can probably be one of the hardest things to deal with as a leader, especially if you are up against staff that do not like what you are trying to achieve.

Now you have your vision as a team, you may find that not all the staff are happy with the changes that may have to occur from this.

Being a leader or manager in early years can be a very stressful job. A lot of different things can be 'thrown' at you on a regular basis, therefore, having resilience has to be part of what makes an 'ultimate leader.'

There will be times when you will need to make changes and developments. We all know that some staff do not like change, and you can be up against staff resistance or some staff being against what you are trying to achieve. Having the resilience to deal with this is so important. This chapter will hopefully give you some guidance on how to tackle this.

There are two types of change.

Change to government policy. This is usually much easier to lead within your setting as it is 'not your fault.' Change to government policy must be accepted by everyone and it is your job to get your staff team to help you with ideas on how to put these changes in place and make the best out of the situation. Sometimes change has to happen. We need to move on with the times. For example, over the past few years, at least, there have been so many developments in technology and different software programmes have been brought in. The idea behind them all is to save us time and to save us on our paperwork; programmes such as 'Tapestry', 'My Concern' for your safeguarding requirements etc. Introducing a change like this can be hard if you have staff that do not want to 'move with the times.'

Which leader role will you need to make this change? Think about the steps you will want to take with this kind of situation and how you get the staff team involved and on board.

The second type of change is from a development that you, as the leader, wants to make. It may be part of your overall vision that you created as a team. There may be many reasons you want to make a change. Some of your team members may have different views on this and see you as the 'enemy' here. So, the way you approach this, matters. You have to plan carefully every step from day one, as you want your team on board.

The changes to the EYFS may have led you to want to make some changes to your curriculum and learning approach. You may have the 'want' to make changes but might be too scared to do it, so you and your team continue as you always have, as it is the easier thing to do.

Staff members that cannot cope very well with 'change' have the opposite of resilience. They feel vulnerable. They try to remove themselves from the stress of change as much as possible, instead of dealing with it. They are too vulnerable and lack courage, motivation, or strategies to make the stressful changes work for them. Instead, they shut down.

It can be tempting to avoid workplace pressures and deny or ignore them. It is not possible to live a life without change. If every day, every month, nothing changes, nothing new happens, boredom and emptiness can set in with your job role. Sometimes change brings excitement with it.

Maybe this could be why you are currently feeling demotivated at the moment, maybe your role has become monotonous. We owe it to the children that we look after, to make appropriate developments. Change must be seen as a positive.

In order for yourself to deal with change and to support your team in this situation, you need what we will call the 3 C's. The 3 C's are: Commitment, Control, and Challenge. These will give you the courage and motivation that is necessary to use in stressful situations- to your advantage.

Commitment

You need to see your role as valuable and important. It needs your imagination and creativity. When a change needs to be made or you want to make a change for the goodness of your setting, then you need to believe that this will work and be committed. How can you be creative to make it work for you and your team? Before sharing it with your team, you need to be confident in the 'why' and the purpose of the development.

You need to stay connected with your team and the actions to achieve the goal. Even when it gets tough. If you are trying to make a change and you have a staff member who is against this, then try to understand how they are feeling and why. Work with them a bit more so that they can gain an understanding of how it can work for them.

Control

Try to solve the problems you are facing and keep calm. It is so important that you stay in control, and you show your team that you are in control. Don't allow yourself to fall into helplessness but try to solve your problems. You need to decide where your efforts need to go. Believe in your strengths and abilities to solve the problem.

Challenge

Can you see change as a way to open up new and fulfilling paths for you? You need to have that positive attitude and mindset that we have talked about in previous chapters. Turn the "I can't" into "I cans." You need to face up to stressful situations and accept them rather than ignore them. For example, if you have a member of staff that is showing they are not happy with the change, then don't ignore this and hope that it will go away. You need to tackle it. You need to be in control. The rest of your staff team will feel more secure if they can see that you are in control and tackling this.

Let's use an example here of how you may implement a change.

Your headteacher or nursery owner tells you that there is a change that needs to happen in your department. It might be staff reductions or a change to a policy. You could choose to go straight to your team and let them know while you are still coming to terms with it yourself:

"You never guess what now, I have just been told this.... What are we going to do?"

Can you see how approaching it this way will instantly show your team that you are not in control. This will cause more stress and anxiety for you and your team down the line.

Instead, take a deep breath and begin to think about the possible implications of these changes for you and your team and for the setting as a whole, perhaps write them down first. Think about the positive opportunities that this may bring. Attempt to predict the problems that your team may have and how you can overcome these.

This will allow you to take appropriate effective action to deal with the changes. You show a commitment, you are in control and accept the challenge in a positive way. Instead of seeing the problem as a challenge, see it as an opportunity.

Another example might be, as a leader, you want to find a better pedagogy to your early years setting. So, you first spend some time researching different learning approaches. You have a vision in your head, you have some ideas of what your team may want, and you think about how each approach could work in your set up. (This is what I did when I came across the Curiosity Approach) You find the perfect one! This gives you excitement and you start to feel inspired and motivated to make the change. However not all your team may feel the same and so if not handled correctly, this can instantly cause you to be de motivated. The first thing you need to do is be confident in why this is the approach for your setting. Why is this the one over all the others? What will this approach mean for your setting, what will the outcomes be? This will show that you have commitment to the development.

In order to be in control, start to think ahead about the problems and concerns that your team may have and how you can iron this out straight away. For example, will they be given the time to learn and understand the reasoning behind it. How will they learn about the approach? Will they have the resources available to do their job? What will the transition be like to change your learning approach? What roles will staff play in this? Show your commitment as a leader, by thinking about the feelings of your team and what their worries maybe. Preplanning this, will show them you are in control. You are aware of what the challenges are going to be, but you have been creative in thinking of ways to overcome them.

If you have a small team, you may decide that the best way to introduce this change is through a full staff meeting. This can be pre planned but have all the information ready. You also have answers to those questions that you think you may be asked. If you have a large team, you may decide to introduce this to your most senior staff members first. It is important that they are on board and show commitment to the change. Any problems in this stage need to be ironed out before introducing it to the wider team. You will then have the support when approaching it to the rest of the team.

The next stage is to involve your team. Making them involved in any change is so important.

You can be strong and positive in your attitude towards challenge. This will help you to stay motivated even through stressful changes.

Non resilient staff are those that act negatively to change. They react negatively to any loss of support. Any disruption to routine or order is seen as a disaster and a sign they aren't valued and being pushed around. They find it harder to spot opportunities, to appreciate them and value them. These staff members can cause problems in a workplace and I think we can all relate to this.

Because they can't manage change effectively, they feel weak and powerless. They may become rigid to gain control and mastery. They may begin to see you as their enemy. People around them will start to suffer.

You must see the 'mood hoover' and deal with the situation, regardless of your fear. Following the 3 c's, being resilient and positive will motivate you and help you see the opportunities in change and take necessary steps to help your team too.

If you show you value and help others, in turn they will trust and value you.

For your own professional development, it might be good for you to reflect on an occasion when you have had to deal with leading a change in your setting. How did you cope with the challenges? How did you lead the change? How did you interact with your team?

Use this to assess how you felt you coped with the experience so that you can learn and grow. This will help you be prepared for any future problems.

Chapter Summary:

- Think about the 3c's; Commitment, Control and Challenge when leading a change in your setting

- Develop your resilience and have a positive attitude when dealing with your team

- When you next have to lead a change in your setting, work your way through your 3C's in order to deal with any negativity from staff members.

Chapter 5
Staff well-being

"On a team, it's not the strength of the individual players, but it's the strength of the unit and how they all function together"

Bill Belichick

The well-being of our team has always been an important subject, but even more now since Covid. When the pandemic hit us in early 2020, some settings closed but other settings and schools carried on. I don't think people appreciated how hard it was for us. During this time, you all had to work harder than normal with the added fear that you may get Covid yourself. Not only did we have to think about how we can keep things normal for our 'key worker' families, but we had to adapt our buildings, purchase more PPE, home educate the children that weren't in, deliver food to some families, the worries of maintaining staffing levels, with the added financial pressure that if you had been in close contact with someone you would have to have possibly, up to two weeks off work! All of this took its toll and people became more aware of how important it was to look after staff well-being and people's mental health. Moving on from Covid times, we are still feeling the pressure. This is why I feel that staff well-being needs to play a big part of being an 'ultimate early years leader.'

As well as the children we look after, the adults also need to feel a 'sense of belonging.' Part of the curiosity approach includes the New Zealand based pedagogy and curriculum; Te Whāriki. The values that underpin this curriculum should be

' to create confident learners and communicators, that have a secure sense of belonging....'

Early Child Curriculum, New Zealand Ministry of Education.

It is also important to extend this ethos to include the staff in your team. A good leader will ensure that there is a sense of community and that all staff are treated fairly and respectfully.

Staff need to feel that they belong, they need to feel confident in their role, and inspired. They need to feel connected to each other. So how can we achieve this? I'm afraid some token biscuits or cakes in the staff room every now again will not be enough.

Although this helps, there needs to be a lot more to how you look after your team members. The feeling of belonging, of shared values and a deep sense of empathy, dramatically enhances trust, cooperation and problem solving within a team.

We have talked previously about how to set your vision together, so you are all working towards the same goal, but this chapter goes deeper into this.

Staff communication

Think about ways that are best to communicate with your staff team. There are a variety of ways that this can be done: closed Facebook groups, WhatsApp groups, emails, memos, notices in the staff room etc. Different methods have their positives and negatives and what works well for some settings, may not work well for others.

Closed Facebook group

This could work well if all your team are on Facebook. You may have some that are not and would not appreciate being told to use social media if they are not comfortable to do so. Closed Facebook groups are good for sharing inspirational posts and photos, but you cannot always attach documents to the post. The administrative side of this can be quite tricky as you need to make sure you have all the correct privacy settings so outsiders cannot join.

WhatsApp group

Everyone loves a WhatsApp group. These are safe to use as the administrator adds the phone numbers of the people to join. If you decide to have a WhatsApp group together, then decide on the rules. They can become more of a social conversation group rather than for notices. You also need to appreciate your staff's own time away from work. In our setting we are a large team and so we now have one called 'staff notice board' which is just for messages and notices and don't need anyone to respond on them if they do not wish to. We then have other sociable groups for other things.

Emails

Emails are a good and convenient system to use to send out notices and documents to read. We use a programme that sends documents and notices to all the staff, and they then tick a box to let us know that they have read it. Make sure you get all your staff members email address' so that you have the option of emailing them when needed. This way is good to share notices but not so easy to share an inspirational post or photos.

· · ·

Memos and notices

This would have been the main method of communication, that we used a few years back. However, placing a memo in a certain place such as the staff room, does not guarantee that everyone will see it or read it. Not everyone may use the staff room in their break time and so finding a place where everyone would see it was very tricky. This may work if you are a small team or you are a room leader and so you could keep it on a board in your room or give a copy to each staff to read.

Whatever method you decide on is down to your individual team needs, but it Is Important to have a system where all staff can receive messages and information at the same time.

Staff values

How can you create a community culture within your staff team?

When we have a sense of belonging, it enables us to feel valued, improves staff health, their happiness, and their motivation.

The first thing to do is to agree a set of staff values together. You could ask your members of staff to write a list of values that they all feel are important and then gather them in, to see which ones are the most popular. If you have a large staff team and you find yourself with a long list of different values, you could give the list back out and ask all your team members to vote for 10 they feel are most important. Then add up the scores and use the 10 that were most voted for. Display these values around their environments to remind them. Values could include; trust, kindness, support, respect, inspired etc.

To keep these values relevant and as a reminder to the team, you could select a different value each month and focus on this with different quotes, ideas, activities or articles etc within your staff room, Facebook group, WhatsApp groups, however you communicate as a team.

What is it like to be a member of staff here?

Have you ever asked yourself what it must feel like to be a member of staff within your team? Now that you have reflected on the different leadership approaches you use in different situations, how does that make your individual staff feel?

You could start off by giving your team a questionnaire to see how they feel? You need to ask them questions about whether they feel that they are treated well, supported and that they have all the things they need to carry out their job role properly.

If you would like to use the format that I have created, then please email me sarah@

sarahputlandearlyyearsconsultancy.co.uk and put 'Book Downloads' as the subject.

You might want staff to complete this activity anonymously so that they feel they can be honest. Whatever the results, you cannot be offended or disheartened. You are doing this activity for a reason: you want to make changes and make a difference. If you use my downloadable format, then in an ideal world you would like all the answers to be 'yes.' If the majority say no to a certain question, then you know where you need to start with your developments. For example, for the professional development question, if the majority of your team answered no for this, then you know you need to think how you can change this. What Professional Development is out there for your team to access? Do they know where to find it? Can you add a section on Professional Development in your supervision format? It might be something simple that you need to do, to make a difference.

Staff room spaces

Have your team got a comfortable and well thought out space to have their breaks? This is so important. In our sector, breaks are short, and the days are so long. It is therefore so important to make every minute count. For example, do your staff have access to instant boiling water for a hot drink? Or do they have to wait around for a kettle to boil? Do you provide tea, coffee and milk (thinking about allergies too) and make sure you are always stocked up well? Do they have comfortable seating? Does it feel homely? Do they have a sense of belonging in this space? I am surprised at how many nurseries do not have a designated staff room or space for one. In schools, sometimes the staff room can be so big that they may lack that cosy/ comfortable feeling. What is your current staff room like?

When we created our staff room, we added elements of Zen and Hygge in the space. Our staff team have access to instant hot water for tea, coffee or hot chocolate. Blankets are available on the backs of chairs if they want to make themselves more comfortable. The room has air con and heating so that the temperature can be comfortable all year round. Within the staff room space, we have a 'book swap' that was set up by some of the team that enjoy reading in their spare time. There are also lots of reference books available for their own professional development.

These are all things for you to think about for your team. If you do not have access to a separate space, then think about a space that can be used at a particular time of day. Is there a room that can be used if the children are outside or asleep? If there is, try and think of a quick turn around for the space. This will show your team that you care about their well-being and comfort.

. . .

Professional Development of your team

Supporting your staff team with their own professional development is another way to show them that you care and support their own well-being. Remember from chapter 1, how important it is to look after your intellectual needs. Professional development can be discussed during supervisions or at other times. It is important to gain an understanding of the interests of your staff team and where they need to develop further, but also, where they would like to develop further. Professional Development isn't always about sending somebody on a course, or for them to do training. Professional Development hours can be built up by reading articles, or watching a video, maybe researching something etc. It can be done in many ways. Just like our children have different learning behaviours that we need to plan for, this is the same with the adults too.

We look at the Professional Development of your team within 'The Ultimate Early Years Leader's Programme.'

Staff supervisions

The statutory requirements say:

'Providers must put appropriate arrangements in place for the supervision of staff who have contact with children and families. Effective supervision

provides support, coaching and training for the practitioner and promotes the interests of children. Supervision should foster a culture of mutual support, teamwork and continuous improvement, which encourages the confidential discussion of sensitive issues.'

The Statutory Framework for the Early Years Foundation Stage

If you are based in a school, then supervisions still need to be done but they may be called something else such as 'performance management meetings.' Whatever system you use, time will no doubt be a big problem. It is not always easy to take a member of staff out of the classroom during the day due to ratios needing to be maintained. But having a system in place is so important and a must. Supervisions support staff's well-being as it allows them to discuss any concerns or 'niggles' that they may have. It is also a good opportunity to praise them and remind them of their achievements so far and what they do well. It makes your team feel listened to. Supervisions don't need to take a lot of time to do but are very effective when done correctly.

You need to aim to see each member of staff every 6-8 weeks. It is worth having a draft plan across the month or term, (depending how your setting operates) as to which staff members you would like to speak to each week. If you only have a small staff team, then this may just be one member of staff to see over the week. Think about the times of day that are less busy or use the time if you have some children that sleep. If you are in a school this may need to be planned for at the end of the school day. In chapter 7 we discuss how to organise your working week to make the most out of your time.

Workload

As a leader you need to make sure that your team have the least amount of paperwork to complete. Keep an eye on their workload and make sure that you ask them how it is within their supervisions. The introduction to the revised EYFS recognised that not all the paperwork was needed anymore. It is up to the individual settings and schools to work out what paperwork is necessary and what isn't. As long as you can prove your impact, it is up to you. Make sure you are not asking your team to complete unnecessary paperwork that has no purpose. This will involve looking at your planning cycle. More nurseries and reception classes are moving over to planning in the moment which is saving a lot of time and meaning that the staff are more with the children getting to know them. What do you expect your staff to show for assessment purposes- do you ask for a certain number of observations each week, for each child? Or do you offer a focus child system, which allows you to only focus on 10% of the children each week? The main thing is that you can show evidence of the impact, that children are making progress and you can recognise which areas children need support with. It might be worth looking at your current paperwork systems to look at what is necessary and important and what can be relaxed. This will show your team that you are supporting them and acknowledging how hard they work.

We look at 'workload' within one of the modules of 'The Ultimate Early Years Leader programme.' For more information visit: www.sarahputlandearlyyearsconsultancy.co.uk

New staff

What is it like to be a new member of staff at your nursery or school? How do you make them feel from the start and what do you do for them to gain a sense of belonging?

You need to have a detailed staff induction in place. An induction should not just be a short tick list that is quickly done on day one. An induction can last over a week, or longer, where each day you concentrate on a different area. Imagine how much a new member of staff needs to know about your setting, including your vision, any learning approaches you may follow, as well as policies and procedures and lots more. You cannot expect somebody to take all this information in at once. Even if the new member of staff is experienced, you can't just throw them into a room and expect them to know how everything operates. Do you offer a workplace mentor for all staff when they start? Have a look at your current induction method. When was this last updated? Does it now need to be updated, to include your new vision and staff values?

How do you give a new member of staff the sense of belonging within your setting? One idea is to give a 'welcome pack.' This can include a 'welcome card' from yourself, and access to any 'communication' methods you have in place, such as a closed Facebook group. Your welcome pack could include items to help them in their first week, such as hand sanitiser, pen, keyring and locker key, a mug for the staff room etc. Think of different ways you can make a new member of staff feel welcomed into your team.

Being a manager or leader can be very hectic, stressful and can be lonely. It is important to make sure that as a nursery manager you have a deputy and as a year group leader or team leader, you have somebody that supports you. If you do not have named deputies, this can be a colleague that you can support you. Someone needs to be looking out for you too and recognising when things are getting a bit much and stepping in to help and support. Do not be afraid to ask people for support and to delegate.

Make well-being part of your team culture. Make it part of everyday things that you do. It can be part of every staff meeting, supervision, inset days and discussed within your policies and procedures. As I said at the beginning of this chapter, it is not enough to just buy some cakes for your staff room, you need to think deeper into their day-to-day roles and what things you can do to help.

How do staff praise each other? Shout out boards, buddy systems are all things that people have incorporated into their routines as a way to praise and support each other. Staff well-being baskets are great to introduce too. Add little items to show that you care. We always have well-being baskets in our staff toilet areas, but they are also introduced at other times of the year in classrooms and staff rooms. What things can you introduce to look after your team's well-being?

Chapter summary:

- Give you staff a set of reflective questions to complete (this can be my questionnaire or you can use your own)
- Use the results to plan developments that need to be made so that they feel supported.
- As a team, set your staff values and display these around the setting to remind all staff
- Think about how you support staff well-being in other areas, for example, staff room, supervisions, and workload.

Chapter 6
Getting Organised

"Getting organised is a sign of self-respect"

Gabrielle Bernstein

Now that you are clear on your own goals and you have a clear vision for your team, you can move on to the next stage……making time!

How do you create the time to fit everything in? Being a leader or a manager comes with lots of different things to cover each day, week, month, and term. Throw in staff illness, an unhappy parent, or a safeguarding concern, and everything gets thrown out of the window.

How often have you gone into work with an idea of what you want to get done in your day, arriving to a situation that means everything must be put on hold as you now have other things you need to prioritise, or you have to teach a class, or be counted in ratios for the day? This leads you feeling very frustrated.

There is no doubt about it, you need to be organised. You need to have an organisation system in place that works for you. The next two chapters are about organisation and some tips on how to begin to organise your time. Organisation systems must be part of being an 'ultimate Early Years leader.'

Where to begin

You might think that this stage is not necessary, but it is so important to have a clear organised system in place. Give it a try and see what happens.

You need to start with your office or desk area. Your workspace needs to be a special place for you to be in. If your office is cluttered and a mess, then you are not going to be able to focus on your work and things will take you a lot longer to do. You may feel like you do not have time to do this right now, but it is so important to invest the time now as it will help you in the long run.

When early years settings are created or designed, office space can be an afterthought. You may have a nice sized office space to use, a shared office, or you may have a very inappropriate sized space and in an area of the nursery or school that is also not appropriate. Whatever shape or size you have, I am hoping that these tips will help.

I have mentioned the art of Zen earlier in the book. Zen is a philosophy that was born out of Mahayana

Buddhism in the 11th Century. It focuses on mindfulness and your mental well-being. It gives you time and space for happiness, health and most importantly love. It is so important to understand how to think clearly and prevent you from getting those high stress levels that we can all relate to.

So how can we incorporate Zen into our daily lives as an early year's manager or leader?

As a manager or leader in a setting you can spend a lot of time, within your day, in your office. You have so many things to juggle on a daily basis; emails, phone calls, admin, invoices, funding, registering new children, recruitment, supervisions, collating data.... The list is endless. You will also use it as a space where you talk to staff and parents, carry out supervisions, and other meetings. If your office area is organised and calm, this shows you to be a good role model and in control. It is therefore so important that Zen is incorporated into your office space.

One of the principles of Zen is simplicity or the elimination of clutter. Having an organised and clear office helps to organise your mind. Your office needs to be a happy place for you to be in. Your desk or office space should inspire you to be more productive and creative.

Have you heard of the 'home edit'? I want us to think about the 'office edit!'

It is worth putting the time in to declutter and organise, to think of a system that will work for you. Office spaces can come in all shapes and sizes. Whether you have a small office that can just about fit a desk and chair or whether you are lucky enough to have a larger space, the following tips can help you.

Having an organised and uncluttered desk allows you to focus on what matters without getting distracted. Visual noise can be very distracting for you. Let's think about how we can keep our office spaces calm and organised.

1. If you have natural daylight in your office space, then plants are so important to have. They reduce stress, help increase productivity and make a space look attractive. If you do not have any space on your desk or floor, then think about having some hanging from the ceiling or on shelves. Being at one with nature is an important principle of Zen. Zen gardens are also very therapeutic if you have space within your office. I place Zen gardens in our staff room and meeting room.
2. Sunlight is naturally uplifting and can help you feel alert. If you have natural light, then use it effectively. Don't put your desk in the direct sunlight as this won't help. Think about the best place to put your desk. Have desk lamps instead of big overhead lighting or strip lighting. This can make your office feel more

cosy, especially in the winter months (and can use less electricity too!)
3. Think about the things that you need on your desk. You will need space for your computer or laptop. (If you use a computer a lot, then it is advised to have your screen raised to your eye level.) Think about what type of keyboard and mouse you are more comfortable working with. Even though I use a laptop, I still prefer to have a Bluetooth mouse to use instead of the mouse pad. At this stage, I have to admit that I have a stationary fetish! Think about the stationary items that you need access to each day. These should be the only ones on your desk or near to your desk. I have to place my other items in my desk drawer or on shelving close by in order to give me the working space that I need. An element of Zen is 'simplicity.' Having too many things in a small space can feel like 'baggage that is weighing you down.' Think carefully about what you actually need to have on your desk and what other types of storage you can use within your space.
4. We are not all blessed with having a big office space, so make good use of the space that you do have (One of my offices was a hallway that we built a small stud wall around!) Even small spaces can work. Find the best place for your desk – thinking about what we said about natural light. What size desk have you

got? Slim line desks can be just as affective in a work space.

'Arrange your room simply. A lifestyle of simplicity is what is beautiful. This is the spirit of Zen.'

1. We have mentioned previously the importance of having a 'Sense of belonging,' not just for children in your environments, but for the other spaces that you and your team use too. Take ownership of your desk space by adding some personal photos or artwork. This can create an uplifting and inspiring place to work. Add inspiring quotes or words. You may like to display your vision or your 'why' so that you can be reminded every day, allowing self-reflection.
2. What colour scheme do you have in your office space? Bright colours will over stimulate you, and paler, more neutral colours will give you a sense of 'calm.' Avoid having lots of different colours or bright colours in your office space. This will only cause visual noise and distraction. You want your work space to feel as homely and calm as possible.

Zen is about habits and ideas for living a happy and calm life. Why not try these things and see if it makes a difference.

Now that you have your office or your desk space how you want it, it is time to come up with an organisation system for all your paperwork. In the next chapter, we will go through a system that I use and find very effective.

Chapter summary:

- Look at your work space and make the time to get it organised.
- When organising your office / desk space think about lighting, nature and a sense of belonging; incorporating Zen as much as possible.

Chapter 7
A Leader's Organisation system

" A good system shortens the road to the goal."

Orison Swett Marden

Time is so valuable to us each day, so it is so Important to be organised. You need a system that works and gives you more time to do all the parts of your job that you love to do.

If you are a nursery manager or leader, the amount of paperwork is unbelievable. You need systems in place for Health and Safety, funding, evidence for Ofsted, administrative work, staff information, including supervisions, appraisals, assessment data.... The list is endless.

Now that you have an organised workspace, that is not enough. You need a system to maintain it otherwise you will always end up back at 'square one.'

Having an organisation system for your workload needs to be part of your role of being a leader. I have created a planner called 'The Early years Leader Planner' that does go alongside this system. (This will be available on Amazon and through my website from October 2022) Alternatively, you can create your own.

In David Allen's book 'Getting things done' he talks about a system for stress free productivity. No matter what our job role there is a 5-step method for managing your workflow. I have taken his suggestion to create a system that fits in with our sector.

In order to begin this method, you will need the following:

- An 'In tray' that will be placed on your desk (now you have space for it) or in your office.
- A 'Current actions' folder to keep the things that you are currently working on
- A folder labelled 'someday/maybe'- this can be a box file or a ring binder
- A planner system- this could be an electronic device (an app on your phone or ipad), a bullet journal method (I highly recommend Yop and Tom journals: https://www.amazon.co.uk/Limited-Curiosity-Approach-Dotted-Journal) or another type of planner. The planner I have designed, fits in with this system and will be available from Amazon or through my website from October.

- Spare folders, ways of labelling and poly pockets.

As you prepare your system, we will break it down into yearly, monthly, weekly and daily.

Yearly

Look at the year ahead and put in any important dates. You may pre-book inset days, staff meetings, governor meetings, parent's evenings, important assessment dates etc. You may have a ritual of celebrating staff birthdays, so you may want to add those in too.

In my planner, I have purposely not added month names and dates in, this is so you can start your planner at any time during the year. There is nothing worse than purchasing a good planner, mid academic year and then only being able to use it for a few months before having to buy a new one.

In chapter 1 you would have set yourself a goal for the year. Have a place at the beginning of your planner / journal to write this down with the steps on how this can be achieved.

Add in your setting's mission statement / your 'why', to remind you of where you are going.

Create a page called 'project list.' If you have something that will take two or more steps to complete, then I would call this a project, rather than an action. So as the time goes on, if there is a 'project' that you need to complete or something that you would like to do, add it on your project list. This will then be broken down and planned for later on.

These initial pages are a way that you can get things out of your head and written down; having a system that gives you regular opportunities to clear your mind.

Monthly

If you are working with a journal or a planner, then create a monthly overview page at the start of each month. On your monthly overview page, add in those important dates, deadlines, or events that you will have. Use these to set some goals for the month. Prepare your monthly page and make note of the goals that you want to achieve during this time (these could be personal, or work based).

In chapter 1 you reflected on your physical, emotional, intellectual, and spiritual needs. These could be included in the things that you would like to achieve in the month ahead.

As a leader, every month there will be different tasks that you do/plan such as a staff meeting, supervisions, professional development activities etc. In your monthly section think about how you can make notes and collect evidence of all these activities. (or you may decide to keep this the evidence somewhere separate)

Projects

At the beginning of a month, you may decide that you would like to start one of those projects on your list. On a new page, give your project a title, summary of what you want to achieve and then break this down into smaller steps. These small steps can then start to be migrated over to your weekly planning as the month goes on.

Weekly

When do you start planning for the week ahead? Do you do this on a Monday morning or before? I always take a short amount of time on a Sunday to give myself a draft plan for the week ahead. This is not in any great detail (as you never know what is going to happen over the week!), it is just to give you an idea of meetings, or deadlines that are coming up.

At the start of each week, you need a fresh 'Actions list.' This is the space where you add any jobs that need to be done. As the week goes on, and you get more actions to complete, add these on. Think of a way that you can show when an action is complete. I always add a small square next to each action and put a cross in it, when complete. There is nothing more satisfying than crossing off completed actions.

As the week goes on you will be handed paperwork, given messages on post it notes, given handouts from meetings or trainings- all of these need to be placed in your in tray. That way you know where everything is until you have the time to sort through it.

Tip: Have a two-minute rule. If something will take you two minutes or less to complete, then do it there and then and get it out of the way.

At some point during the week, you will need to get your in tray to zero. Select a time that works best for you. Depending on how much you have collected over the week this could take 30 minutes up to 60 minutes to complete. I always do this on my last working day of the week, so I have a fresh start for the new week.

Getting your in tray to zero

Now you have everything in the right place, it is time to work out what to do with it. This does not mean you have to complete all the actions, or jobs that are in the tray, it just means that you are giving everything a place.

At this point you will need your 'current actions' folder to hand. This is the place that you keep all the relevant paperwork to go alongside your actions list in your planner. You will also need your 'Someday/maybe' folder. You may be asking yourselves what on earth is this. This folder is for all those things that you may wish to do if you ever had the time. With all these steps in place, you will start to have more time and so you can then start to use the things in this folder.

You have your in tray in front of you. With each item in the tray, you need to ask yourself the following question:

What is it? Is it actionable? If the answer is no, then ask yourself what you want to do with it.

- Bin it / shred it
- Put it in your 'someday/maybe' folder to look at, at a later date
- Or in another relevant folder

If the answer is yes, then what is the next step?

- If it will take you less than two minutes to complete, do it straight away
- Delegate it to someone else
- Defer for you to do yourself, by adding it on to your actions list and putting the document in your 'current actions' folder. If it has a deadline or a specific date, then add this onto your monthly, or weekly overview too.

Go through the tray and ask these questions for each item. The idea is to get your tray to empty. Everything has now been allocated a place in your actions list. Watching your tray get higher and higher each week will automatically make you feel stressed, just by looking at it. It is so important to get this empty, for your own mental well-being.

You will work through your actions list as the week goes on. Any items that you have not completed at the end of the week, can just be migrated to the following week's actions list. Make sure you are not overloading your actions list- be realistic to yourself about what you are physically and mentally able to do each week. I give myself a goal of having 2-3 main actions a day. So, this would mean that I try to not add more than 10-15 actions a week. If you find yourself with a lot less, then you go to your projects list or your 'someday/ maybe' list and start to work on something new.

Emails

Emails can be a very demanding part of your role. Everyday things come into your inbox that you feel the pressure to answer straight away. Just like having a system for your paperwork, you need to have a system for your emails too.

Set up folders within your email, these could be labelled with whatever you feel is necessary. I have the following:

- A 'someday/ maybe' one, which works in the same way as the paper version
- A 'current actions' one, that you work through each week, or you may just flag or star the current emails to work on if easier
- If I have an event coming up such as parents evening, then all relevant emails go into this folder etc.

The same principle applies as your in tray. Have a rule to only check your emails at certain times of the day and then close them down in between (unless you are waiting for an urgent one). If you have emails consistently on then every time you see you have a number appear in the brackets, you will be tempted to stop what you are doing and have a look. This can be very distracting. This is what I suggest you do:

- Check emails first thing in the morning but scan for emergency emails or things you need to know about straight away, such as a child's absence. If an email will take two minutes or less to reply to, then quickly do it. Anything else that needs longer can be starred and flagged or moved to the 'current actions' folder for a later time.

- Check emails mid-morning and mid-afternoon, and do the same

Tip: We live in a world that is fast paced and instant. This has added to our pressure to reply to an email almost instantly. In order to relieve this pressure, you could encourage parents to call the setting if they have a question or make use of your 'out of office autoreply.' Maybe add a message saying something like 'please allow us 2 working days to respond to you' or 'all emails are checked regularly and will be responded to within the week.' This gives a clear message to your parents that they may have to wait for a response.

Once a week you need to get your inbox to zero, just like you do with your in tray. Allocate yourself time to do this once a week. During your allocated time slot, go to your flagged, starred, or current actions folder and work your way through them.

Ask yourself 'is it actionable?"

No – then delete it or put it in a relevant folder for a later day

If it is actionable, then you do the following:

- Do it straight away if it will take under two minutes
- Delegate it by forwarding it to the relevant person

- Defer it -place it on your actions list and come back to it when you have the time to.

Every week, I add 'complete starred emails' onto my actions list and set aside between 60 and 90 minutes to complete. Obviously, this can take longer if you have been off work. Our weekend time is so precious to us, and to start our weekends with a clear mind and knowing your in tray and inbox is sorted and organised will definitely help with this.

Mind sweep

I mentioned earlier the importance of doing a mind sweep. Our job roles mean that our brains work on full capacity. We are all so guilty of having many things in our heads at once and this can cause us a lot of issues from not being able to concentrate, not knowing where to start on our long list, focusing on one thing, to having sleepless nights when we lie awake thinking of all the things we need to do. Once a week, (or you may want to do this daily) carry out a mind sweep. Write down all those thoughts you have going round in your head. When you have done this, look at each item and either add it onto your weekly 'action list' or on your 'project list' or anywhere else where it may be relevant to go. When I first qualified as a teacher, a friend of mine bought me a small notebook and pen to keep on my bedside table. She told me to write anything down that was on my mind so that I did not think about it in the night, or if I woke up in the night and thought about something, to write it down at the time. I have always stuck by this rule! You could try this and use the notebook to clear your mind at the end of each day, before you go to bed.

Daily

If you are working in a journal, create a daily page with time slots down the side. Each morning, take a few minutes to plan your day ahead. Your work involves making split second judgements and managing all the ongoing data and information coming at you. This system should help relieve the stress and help you to be more productive.

When you arrive at work, within the first 15 minutes you will know if you have a member of staff off ill, if you need to cover in a room at any point, or if there is a phone message that you will need to deal with etc.

At the beginning of the day, you need to put a draft plan in place. Your daily page needs to have the timings on it, so that you can see at a quick glance when you will have time free. The first step is to review your calendar. Look at what meetings, appointments, or visitors you may have that day and at what time. Add these into the correct time slots on your daily plan. If you are now unable to attend, then contact them to let them know.

Do an emergency scan of your emails to see if there is anything that needs to be dealt with straight away. Do not get distracted by what you see. If there is an email that needs responding to that day, add it on your daily plan.

Are you needed to cover any breaks? Are you on break duty? Add this into the relevant time slot.

By looking at your daily plan you will be aware of what your day ahead looks like. You should then be able to work out when you can be office based. Before planning this in, think about what your energy levels are like at different times of the day? I have my most energy first thing in the morning and I know mid-afternoon my brain does not function very well due to tiredness. I then get another energy boost during late afternoon. This is now my most productive daily routine. Think about when you are most productive and select these times to be in the office if you can, concentrating on paperwork. Select the more practical jobs at other times of the day.

Remember that if you want to have a performance management meeting or supervision with a member of staff this may have to happen at a certain time of the day. Next step is to check your actions list and add items onto your daily list, that will fit in with the times that you have.

Fill in your day with actions but only select 2-3 items from your list and then that way if anything 'crops' up, this should not have a great impact on you too much.

There is nothing worse than having the pressure of ten things to do and complete, on an already busy day! You may want to do this in pencil. That way if something 'crops up' you can rub it out. There is nothing worse for your mindset to see lots of things scribbled out or left on your list incomplete.

Remember to set time aside to get your in tray and inbox to zero. You may want to select the day and prewrite it in at the start of the week so you know it is already there.

Think about what time you have and the length of gaps between things. If you have a 20-30 minute slot free, then look through your action list and see if there is anything you can get done within this time.

Being organised with folders and having a good planner is a valuable time saver and stress saver. It enables you to quickly store information in an organised way and quickly find things that you need. Everybody's job roles and settings are different and so the folders that you choose to have, and use will be personal to you. I am sure that you have lots of different folders that you need to use but try to work out which ones you will need access to everyday and which ones can be kept in a cupboard to refer to at other times of the year.

Chapter summary:

- Whether you like my suggested organisation system or prefer your own, it doesn't matter as long as you have something in place
- Look at the different systems that can be used to capture and organise your 'to do's'
- Whatever you choose to use- put something in place to give you the time to do the parts of your job you love.
- Coming Soon! We will be developing a 'shop' through my website for some useful tools and resources

Final Words

" I want to inspire people. I want someone to look at me and say because of you I didn't give up."

Anonymous

We are currently working in a sector that is making people demotivated, stressed, and questioning their chosen career. I can see the stress it is causing us all and I wanted to write this book to hopefully help some of you and to know you are not alone.

Unfortunately, I can't wave a magic wand to sort out the recruitment crisis, I can't stop Covid and staff sickness, I can't give the sector more money for funding and pay, but what I can do is try to help you all find a love for your job again and give you tips and advice on how to make things easier.

If we allow the worries and stresses to take over then it won't help anybody. I wrote this book to help you look at a way to start over again, to change your mindset. To make your vision and goals clearer, to find where your passion is and to find a system that saves you time, resulting in more time for you to spend on the jobs you love doing.

If you want to become an 'Ultimate Early Years Leader' then from here you can have a look through my website to see the other ways that I can offer you for support. I also offer bespoke consultancy sessions, so please just get in touch to ask.

About the Author

Sarah Putland qualified as a teacher in 2001 and has owned her own nursery since 2005.

Sarah is an Ambassador for the Curiosity Approach where she runs different Discovery sessions on a range of all things curious. This is where she found her passion for helping others, and inspiring people to change our early years practise for the good of the unique child. Seeing how the sector is struggling in today's climate, has led her to set up 'Sarah Putland Early Years Consultancy.'

You can connect with Sarah at:

www.sarahputlandearlyyearsconsultancy.co.uk

Facebook: www.facebook.com/Sarah-Putland-Early-Years-Consultancy-106918318765258/

Instagram: @sarahputlandconsultancy

Curiosity Approach Ambassador Facebook: www.facebook.com/curiosityapproachsouthandeastsussex/

Sarah's nursery setting Facebook: www.facebook.com/saffronsparknursery/

Email: sarah@sarahputlandearlyyearsconsultancy.co.uk

If you are interested or want to find out more about the Curiosity Approach then please visit www.thecuriosityapproach.com

Bibliography

Matthew Kelly (2004) The Rhythm of Life: Living Everyday With Passion and Purpose. Beacon Publishing.

Simon Sinek (2017) Find Your Why: A Practical Guide for Discovering Purpose for You and Your Team. Penguin

David Allen (2015) Getting Things Done: The Art of Stress-free Productivity. Piatkus

Nelson Bolles R (2009) How to find your mission in life. Crown Publishing Group.

Printed in Great Britain
by Amazon